How We Use

Glass

Chris Oxlade

www.raintreepublishers.co.uk

Visit our website to find out more information about **Raintree** books.

To order:
- ☎ Phone 44 (0) 1865 888112
- 📄 Send a fax to 44 (0) 1865 314091
- 💻 Visit the Raintree bookshop at **www.raintreepublishers.co.uk** to browse our catalogue and order online.

First published in Great Britain by Raintree,
Halley Court, Jordan Hill, Oxford OX2 8EJ,
part of Harcourt Education.
Raintree is a registered trademark of Harcourt
Education Ltd.

Editorial: Nick Hunter
Design: Kim Saar
Picture Research: Heather Sabel and Amor
    Montes de Oca
Production: Alex Lazarus

Originated by Ambassador Litho Ltd.
Printed and bound in China by South China
Printing Company

ISBN 1 844 43265 3
08 07 06 05 04
10 9 8 7 6 5 4 3 2 1

British Library Cataloguing in Publication Data
Oxlade, Chris
How We Use Glass. - (Using Materials)
620.1'44
A full catalogue record for this book is available from the British Library.

Acknowledgements
The publishers would like to thank the following for permission to reproduce photographs:
ACE p. **7**; Andy Arthur Photography p. **8**; Corbis pp. **4** (Nogues Alain/SYGMA), **5**, **9** (Rodney Hyett/Elizabeth Whiting & Associates), **11** (Bob Rowan/Progressive Image), **12**, **13** (Bob Zaunders), **14** (Maiman Rick/SYGMA), **15** (Bob Krist), **16**, **17**, **18** (William James Warren), **22** (C/B Productions), **24** (James L. Amos), **27** (Alan Goldsmith), **28** (Lewis Alan/SYGMA); Drew Super Photography p. **19**; Getty Images (Stone) p. **29**; Jonah Calinawan p. **23**; Liz King Media p. **25**; pp. Visuals Unlimited pp. **6** (Larry Stepanowicz) **10** (Mark E. Gibson), **21** (Warren Stone) **26** (Inga Spence).

Cover photographs reproduced with permission of Corbis (top) and Corbis (Bob Witkowski) (bottom).

Every effort has been made to contact copyright holders of any material reproduced in this book. Any omissions will be rectified in subsequent printings if notice is given to the publishers.

The paper used to print this book comes from sustainable resources.

Contents

Any words appearing in bold, **like this**, are explained
in the Glossary.

Glass and its properties

All the things we use at home, school and work are made from materials. Glass is a material. It can be used for all sorts of different jobs. For example, we make ornaments from glass, we cover buildings with glass and a type of glass even carries our emails around the world.

Glass lets light into these buildings but keeps out wind and rain.

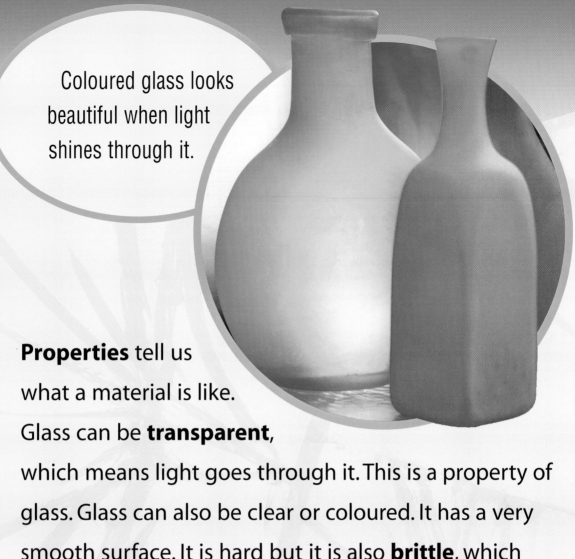

Coloured glass looks beautiful when light shines through it.

Properties tell us what a material is like. Glass can be **transparent**, which means light goes through it. This is a property of glass. Glass can also be clear or coloured. It has a very smooth surface. It is hard but it is also **brittle**, which means it breaks before it bends. Air and water cannot flow through glass and neither can **electricity**.

Don't use it!

The different properties of materials make them useful for different jobs. For example, glass is brittle. It cannot bend without snapping. So we could not use glass to make something that needs to bend, such as a spring.

Where does glass come from?

Glass is not a **natural** material. It is made in factories. The **raw materials** for glass are natural. They come from the ground. The main raw material is sand. It is the same as the sand on a beach. There are different kinds of glass. To make each kind of glass, different **chemicals** are added to the sand. Most glass is soda glass. It is made from sand, limestone and a chemical called soda ash.

Glass is mostly made of sand. Sand is made up of tiny grains of **silica**.

When the liquid glass cools it turns to **solid**, clear glass.

Making glass

At a glass factory the ingredients are mixed together and poured into a huge tank. The glass **mixture** is heated to about 1500 °Celsius, which is many times hotter than the temperature in a kitchen oven. The sand **melts** and mixes with the other ingredients. This makes hot, **liquid** glass.

The history of glass

People discovered how to make small glass things, such as beads, about 4500 years ago. About 2000 years ago glass blowing was invented. This is a way of making hollow glass things such as drinking glasses and vases.

7

Glass windows

Most of the glass made in factories is used in windows. Glass is a good material for making windows because it is **transparent**, **waterproof** and **airtight**. So a glass window lets light in, but it keeps out wind and rain. It also keeps warm air in, stopping a room getting cold. Glass used in windows is called glazing.

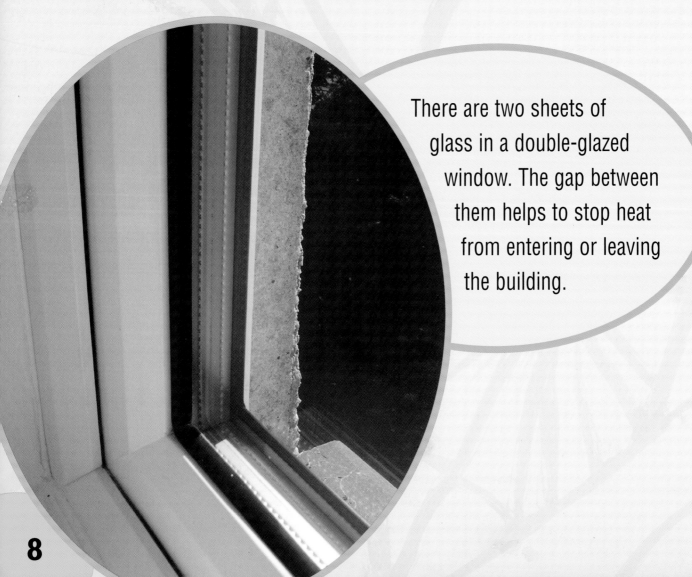

There are two sheets of glass in a double-glazed window. The gap between them helps to stop heat from entering or leaving the building.

Obscure glass is made by blasting the glass surface with sand or by adding patterns.

Rough glass

We do not use plain glass in rooms that we do not want people to see into, such as bathrooms. Instead we use glass with a rough surface, called obscure glass. Obscure glass lets light in, but you cannot see clearly through it.

Making window glass

Windows are made from a type of glass called float glass.

To make float glass, **molten** glass is poured into a huge bath full of a molten metal called tin. The glass spreads out on top of the tin to make a very flat, thin sheet. The sheet is cooled very slowly, which stops it cracking.

Glass in buildings

Some buildings are completely covered in glass. The glass hangs on the outside of the building in huge sheets. It makes the building look like a giant mirror. Some modern houses have glass walls instead of brick walls. This lets plenty of sunlight in, but means that people can see in from outside.

A layer of glass on the outside of a building is called a curtain wall because it hangs like a curtain.

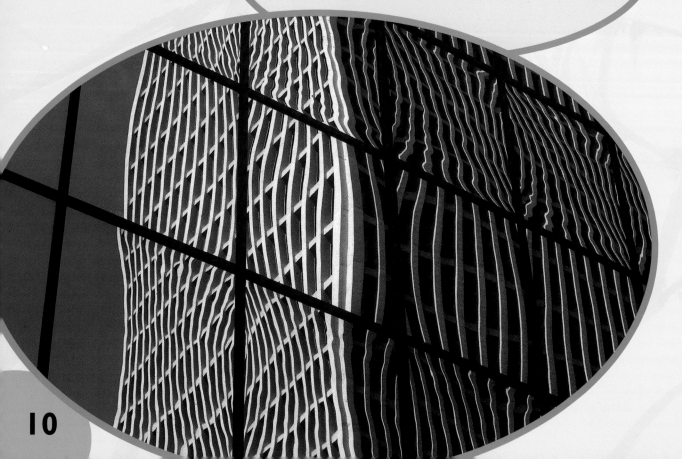

Some walls inside buildings are made of glass, too.

Keeping warm

Skyscrapers and office blocks are often covered in special kinds of glass that look silvery or grey. The Sun gives us heat and light, but harmful rays also come from the Sun. These special kinds of glass let heat and light into the building, but keep out the harmful rays. The glass also stops heat escaping.

Don't use it!

*Glass can cover a building but it cannot hold a building up. Glass is hard but it is also **brittle**. It would break if we used it to build the frame of a building. Other materials, such as concrete and steel, are much better for this job.*

Glass colours and patterns

Many beautiful glass ornaments are made from coloured glass. To make coloured glass, special **chemicals** are added when the glass is made. Different chemicals create different colours in the glass. Light that shines through coloured glass turns that colour too. If you look through coloured glass, you can see to the other side, but everything there looks the same colour as the glass.

A stained-glass window is made up of hundreds of pieces of coloured glass.

An engraving wheel cuts slowly into the glass, making a groove.

Glass engraving

We can draw pictures and patterns on glass by engraving, or cutting into it. Deep lines and curves are cut with a spinning disc. The surface can also be engraved with **acid** that eats away at the glass. This makes the surface look frosty. Engraved glass objects are often made from a sort of glass called lead glass, which is very sparkly.

Glass and heat

When glass is heated to about 600 °Celsius it begins to go soft. The more it is heated, the softer it becomes. When the temperature reaches about 1500 °Celsius the glass is a runny **liquid**. When it cools down it turns back to a **solid** again. Glass can be heated and cooled like this many times.

Bottles are made by pouring molten glass into a mould.

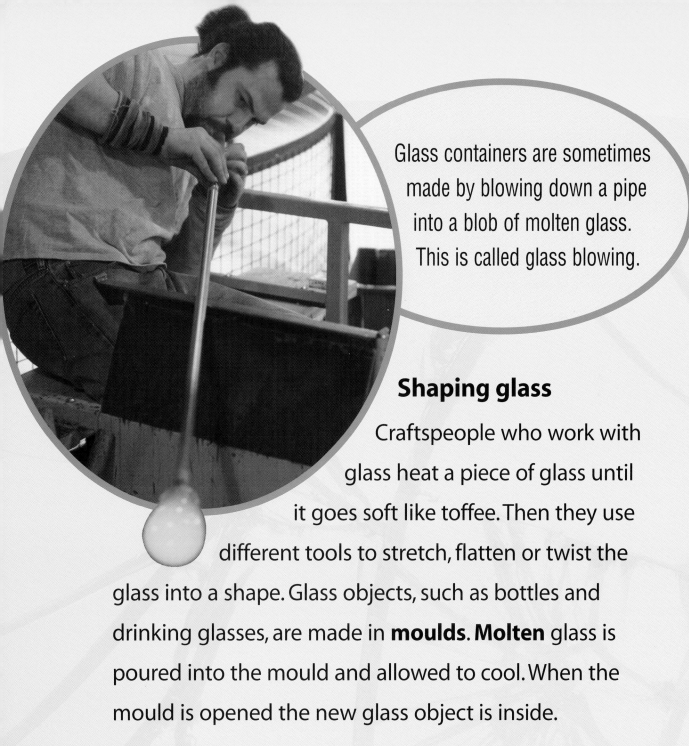

Glass containers are sometimes made by blowing down a pipe into a blob of molten glass. This is called glass blowing.

Shaping glass

Craftspeople who work with glass heat a piece of glass until it goes soft like toffee. Then they use different tools to stretch, flatten or twist the glass into a shape. Glass objects, such as bottles and drinking glasses, are made in **moulds**. **Molten** glass is poured into the mould and allowed to cool. When the mould is opened the new glass object is inside.

Glass for lights

Millions of light bulbs are made from glass every day. The bulbs are made by machines that puff air into small blobs of glass, blowing them up like lumps of bubble gum.

Glass containers

Water and air cannot flow through glass. It is **waterproof** and **airtight**. These **properties** mean it is a good material for making containers such as drinking glasses, jars and bottles. You must be careful with glass containers because they shatter easily if they are dropped.

Glass containers, such as drinking glasses, are made in **moulds** so that they are all the same shape.

A test tube made from borax glass does not crack when it is heated up, even if it glows red-hot.

Chemical containers

Many **chemicals** that scientists use eat away materials such as plastic and metal. These chemicals cannot be stored in plastic or metal containers because the containers would leak. Most chemicals do not affect glass so they can be safely stored in glass containers.

Glass in hot places

*Ordinary glass containers cannot be used for cooking. If they are heated up or cooled down quickly the glass cracks. Cooking containers are made from a special glass called borax glass that does not crack. **Test tubes** used by scientists are also made of borax glass.*

Tough glass

Some types of glass are much stronger than the ordinary glass in windows and bottles. We use tough glass in places where the glass might be hit by something accidentally, such as glass doors and car windscreens. Ordinary glass can shatter into sharp pieces. Tough glass does not shatter like this. If it does break, it breaks into small lumps.

This car windscreen was made from laminated glass. It has cracked but has not fallen into pieces.

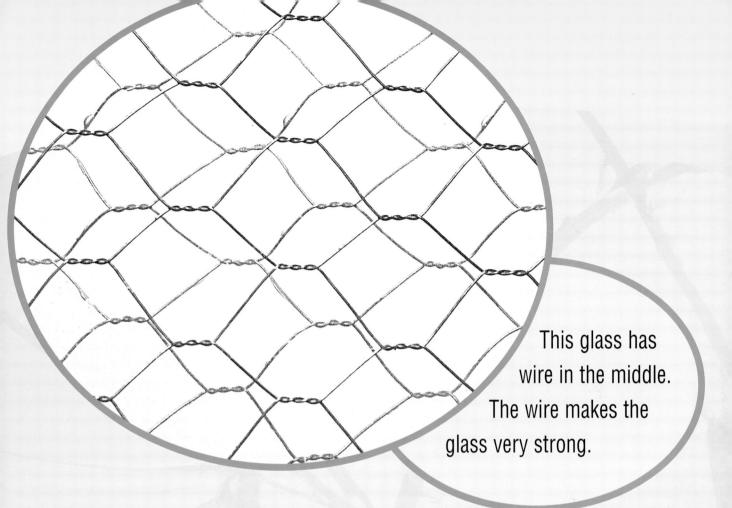

This glass has wire in the middle. The wire makes the glass very strong.

Tempering is a way of making ordinary glass into tough glass. To temper glass, the glass is heated up and cooled down slowly. Glass made by tempering is called toughened glass or safety glass.

Another way of making glass tough is called laminating. A sheet of laminated glass is made up of two sheets of glass with a layer of plastic in between.

Glass mirrors

A mirror is made from a flat sheet of glass with silver paint on the back. When you look in a mirror, light from your face goes through the glass. The light **reflects** off the silver paint, just like a ball bounces off a wall. Then the light comes back through the glass. Because the glass is so flat you see a perfect reflection of your face.

Mirrors show us what we look like.

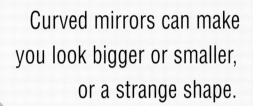

Curved mirrors can make you look bigger or smaller, or a strange shape.

See-through mirrors

Reflecting glass is a sort of flat glass that looks like a mirror. It has a layer of special **chemicals** on the surface. Most of the light that hits the glass bounces off, but a tiny bit goes through. A sheet of reflecting glass looks like a shiny mirror from one side but like normal glass from the other side. Reflecting glass is used to keep bright sunlight out of buildings.

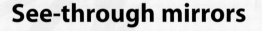

Glass lenses

If you look through a glass object like a bottle or a glass, things the other side look out of shape or blurred. This happens because light from the other side gets bent as it goes into the glass and out again. Scientists use this **property** of glass to make glass lenses. Lenses have curved faces so they bend light.

A magnifier has a glass lens. The glass bends light so that small things look bigger.

The lenses in a pair of glasses help people with poor eyesight to see better.

Devices, such as microscopes, telescopes, binoculars and cameras, have lenses inside. The lenses are curved to make things look bigger or smaller, or to make pictures on a film. Lenses are made from a sort of glass called optical glass. It is very clear so that all the light that hits it goes through.

Plastic lenses

*Glass lenses are expensive to make. Sometimes it is better to use cheaper plastic lenses instead. The plastic bends the light in the same way as glass does. For example, **disposable** cameras have plastic lenses instead of glass lenses. This means that the cameras are cheaper to make and buy.*

Glass fibres

A **fibre** is a very thin piece of material. A glass fibre is a very thin piece of glass. Glass fibres are very strong if you try to pull them apart, but they snap easily if you bend them. We use glass fibres in different ways.

Glass fibres are made by pushing **molten** glass through tiny holes.

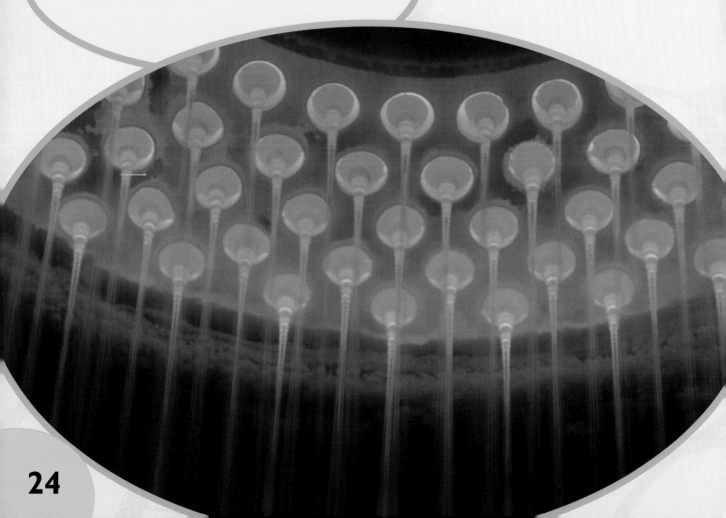

The hull of this boat is made of fibreglass. This is made by pouring plastic over glass fibres.

Glass fibres are made into fabric by **weaving**. Glass fibre fabric does not burn or melt until it gets extremely hot. It is used to make clothes for firefighters and blankets for putting out fires. Glass fibres are also bundled together to make thick, squashy matting. The matting is used for **insulation** in houses. It stops heat escaping from the house.

Mixing with plastic

Glass fibres are mixed with plastic to make a material called glass-reinforced plastic or fibreglass. The glass makes the plastic extremely strong. Glass-reinforced plastic is used to make boats, car bodies and water tanks.

Optical fibres

An optical **fibre** is a special kind of glass fibre. It is made up of a glass fibre with a plastic coating on the outside. If you shine light into one end of an optical fibre the light bounces along the inside of the fibre and comes out the other end. It works even if the optical fibre is bent round a corner.

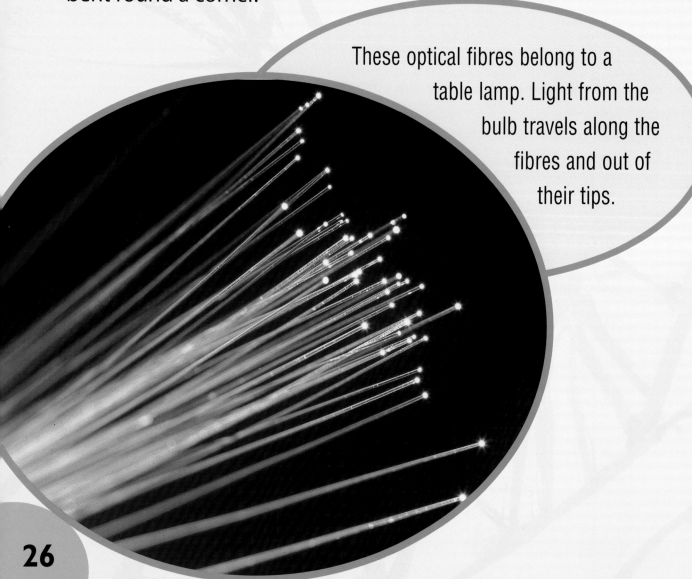

These optical fibres belong to a table lamp. Light from the bulb travels along the fibres and out of their tips.

There are many optical fibres inside an optical-fibre communication cable. The delicate fibres are protected from damage by a plastic coating.

Carrying messages

Optical fibres are very important for communications. Telephone calls, emails and other sorts of information are changed to flashes of light that travel along optical fibres buried underground. The flashes of light travel at the speed of light – 300,000 kilometres (186,000 miles) per second. A message could travel around the world through an optical fibre ten times in just one second! Thousands of telephone calls can travel together along a single optical fibre at the same time.

Glass and the environment

The **raw materials** for glass are plentiful and easy to find. However, it takes a lot of energy to dig them out of the ground and to make them into glass. We can help to save this energy by using the glass again instead of throwing it away. This is called **recycling**. Glass does not **rot** away if we throw it away.

Glass that is not thrown away properly is a danger to people and animals.

It is important to separate used glass into different colours.

How glass is recycled

Most towns have recycling bins where you can put used bottles and jars. The bins are taken to a recycling factory where the glass is crushed and melted to make new glass.

Don't use it!

*Most glass things can be made from recycled glass. However, recycled glass is not pure. We cannot use it in places where we need glass to be very pure such as for lenses and optical **fibres**.*

Find out for yourself

The best way to find out more about glass is to investigate it for yourself. Look around your home for places where glass is used, and keep an eye out for glass through your day. Think about why glass was used for each job. What **properties** make it suitable? You will find the answers to many of your questions in this book. You can also look in other books and on the Internet.

Books to read

Science Answers: Grouping Materials, Carol Ballard (Heinemann Library, 2003)

Discovering Science: Matter, Rebecca Hunter (Raintree, 2003)

Science Files: Glass, Steve Parker (Heinemann Library, 2003)

Using the Internet

Try searching the Internet to find out about things to do with glass. Websites can change, so if one of the links below no longer works, don't worry. Use a search engine, such as www.yahooligans.com or www.internet4kids.com.
For example, you could try searching using the keywords 'glass blowing', 'glass recycling' and 'lenses'

Website

A great site, which explains all about different materials:
http://www.bbc.co.uk/schools/revisewise/science/materials/

A fun site that explains how glass is made and used:
www.glassonweb.com/glassmanual

Glossary

acid liquid that can eat away at materials

airtight describes a material that does not let air pass through it

brittle describes a material that breaks before it bends

chemical substance that we use to make other substances

disposable describes an object that is designed to be thrown away after it is used

electricity form of energy that flows along wires

fibre long, thin, bendy piece of material

insulate stop heat escaping

liquid substance that takes the shape of whatever container it is put into

melt turn from a solid into a liquid by heating

mixture substance made from two or more other substances mixed together

molten melted

mould block of material with a space in the centre. When molten glass is poured into the mould it cools and sets, making an object the same shape as the inside of the mould.

natural describes anything that is not made by people

property quality of a material that tells us what it is like. Hard, soft, bendy and strong are all properties.

raw material natural material that is used to make other materials

recycle to use material from old objects to make new objects

reflect to bounce off. You see yourself in a mirror because light reflects from it.

rot to be broken down

silica substance found in the Earth's surface

solid substance that does not flow

test tube glass tube with an open top and closed bottom

transparent describes a material that lets light pass through it

waterproof describes a material that does not let water pass through it

weaving making fabric by passing lengths of yarn over and under each other

Index

Titles in the *Using Materials* series include:

Hardback   1 844 43260 2

Hardback   1 844 43267 X

Hardback   1 844 43265 3

Hardback   1 844 43263 7

Hardback   1 844 43266 1

Hardback   1 844 43261 0

Hardback   1 844 43262 9

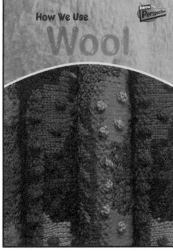

Hardback   1 844 43268 8

Find out about the other titles in this series on our website www.raintreepublishers.co.uk